With love and thanks to my family
for the memories of Christmas past,
the joys of Christmas present, and
the promise of Christmas yet to come.

T.H.


For Bernice, Sadie and Grace.

W.H.

**Waldman House Press**
2300 Louisiana Avenue North, Suite B
Golden Valley, MN 55427

Waldman House Press is an imprint of TRISTAN Publishing, Inc.

Please visit us at:
www.waldmanhouse.com

# A Cup of

# Christmas Tea

by Tom Hegg  illustrated by Warren Hanson

Waldman House Press

The log was in the fireplace,
all spiced and set to burn.
At last, the yearly Christmas race
was in the clubhouse turn.

The cards were in the mail,
all the gifts beneath the tree,
and 30 days reprieve
'til VISA could catch up with me.

And though smug satisfaction
seemed the order of the day,
something still was nagging me,
and would not go away.

$\mathcal{A}$ week before, I got a letter
from my old Great Aunt.
It read: "Of course, I'll understand
completely if you can't...

But if you find you have some time,
how wonderful if we
could have a little chat
and share a cup of Christmas tea."

She'd had a mild stroke that year,

which crippled her left side.

Though housebound now, my folks had said

it hadn't hurt her pride.


They said: "She'd love to see you.

What a nice thing it would be

for you to go and maybe

have a cup of Christmas tea."


But boy! I didn't want to go!

Oh, what a bitter pill

to see an old relation

and how far she'd gone downhill.

I remembered her as vigorous,
as funny and as bright.
I remembered Christmas Eves
when she regaled us half the night.

I didn't want to risk all that.
I didn't want the pain.
I didn't need to be depressed.
I didn't need the strain.

*A*nd what about my brother?

Why not him? She's his *A*unt, too!

*I* thought *I* had it justified,

but then before *I* knew...


The reasons not to go

*I* so painstakingly had built

were cracking wide and crumbling

in an acid rain of guilt.

I put on boots and gloves and cap,
shame stinging every pore,
and armed with squeegee, sand and map,
I went out my front door.

I drove in from the suburbs
to the older part of town.
The pastels of the newer homes
gave way to gray and brown.

$I$ had that disembodied feeling
as the car pulled up
and stopped beside the wooden house
that held the Christmas cup.

How I got up to her door,
I really couldn't tell...
I watched my hand rise up
and press the button of the bell.

I waited,
aided by my nervous rocking to and fro,
and just as I was thinking
I should turn around and go...

I heard the rattle of the china
in the hutch against the wall.
The triple beat of two feet and a crutch
came down the hall.

The clicking of the door latch
and the sliding of the bolt,
and a little swollen struggle
popped it open with a jolt.

She stood there, pale and tiny,
looking fragile as an egg...
I forced myself from staring at the brace
that held her leg.

And though her thick bifocals
seemed to crack and spread her eyes,
their milky and refracted depths
lit up with young surprise.

"Come in! Come in!" She laughed the words.

She took me by the hand,

and all my fears dissolved away,

as if by her command.

We went inside, and then,

before I knew how to react,

before my eyes and ears and nose

was Christmas past...alive...intact:

The scent of candied oranges,
of cinnamon and pine...
The antique wooden soldiers
in their military line...

The porcelain Nativity
I'd always loved so much...
The Dresden and the crystal
I'd been told I mustn't touch...

My spirit fairly bolted,

like a child out of class,

and danced among the ornaments

of calico and glass.


Like magic, I was six again,

deep in a Christmas spell,

steeped in the million memories

the boy inside knew well.

And here, among old Christmas cards,

so lovingly displayed,

a special place of honor

for the ones we kids had made.

$\mathcal{A}$nd there, beside her rocking chair,

the center of it all...

my Great Aunt stood and said

how nice it was I'd come to call.

I sat...and rattled on about
the weather and the flu.
She listened very patiently,
then smiled and said, "What's new?"

Thoughts and words began to flow.
I started making sense.
I lost the phony breeziness
I use when I get tense.

She was still passionately interested
in everything I did.
She was positive. Encouraging.
Like when I was a kid.

Simple generalities
still sent her into fits.
She demanded the specifics.
The particulars. The bits.

We talked about the limitations
that she'd had to face.
She spoke with utter candor,
and with humor and good grace.

Then, defying the reality
of crutch and straightened knee,
on wings of hospitality,
she flew to brew the tea.

I sat alone with feelings
that I hadn't felt in years.
I looked around at Christmas
through a thick, hot blur of tears.

And the candles and the holly
she'd arranged on every shelf...
the impossibly good cookies
she still somehow baked herself.

But these rich, tactile memories
became quite pale and thin
when measured by the Christmas
my Great Aunt kept deep within.

Her body halved and nearly spent,
but my Great Aunt was whole.
I saw a Christmas miracle...
the triumph of a soul.

The triple beat of two feet and a crutch
came down the hall.
The rattle of the china
in the hutch against the wall.

She poured two cups. She smiled,
and then she handed one to me,
and then, we settled back
and had a cup of Christmas tea.